WITHIN YOU

G. P. MUTHU PAVITHRA

"To the people who want their goals and dreams to be achieved"

Contents

FOREWORD

Namaste to all. This book highlights the success tips for our successful life. Moreover stress about the self-analysis and evaluation, steps to be taken for practicing hard work and preparation for success, how to be stronger in our life facing the difficulty and problems. Usage of questionnaires to know about us along with how to transform our dreams into goals which are explained in simple English and short stories are wonderful. The quotes used in various pages of the book are thought-provoking. How to plan for success is being dealt with by the author in a different view is appreciable. The motivating words are highly impressive to the readers. Planning for either short-term or long-term to achieve the goal is depends upon individual awareness and action. Planning for vision, overuse of cell phone effects, the difference between planning and preparation, vision for the future, stress management are all clearly explained in this book. Knowing about our inner power, making changes to move forward, questioning ourselves, and being ready to accept the changes, the positive thoughts for our individual personality development is welcoming. Our mind is an essential feature for our well-being as correctly pointed out by the author. I suggest the readers find happiness by reading the book written by the author and express their feedback to her for future endeavors.

Mr.Gopalakrishnan,
Principal of Aananda Vidyalaya
Mat. Hr. Sec. School, Rajapalayam.

PREFACE

Most of the information I've shared in this book is my own life experience of twenty-two years. As this is my first book I was very much excited to give you the best of my writing. Hope you will like it. This book appeared as the result of the motivation risen within me which I've explained in brief. As we all know the part of human life is nothing without motivation, and the quality of our life lies in our success and how we are succeeded.

The Introduction section of chapter 1 gives you a very brief overview of the plans that you should make for your life, how will you plan it, and how does it work. Also, it talks about the demands of success, tips to be very successful. Chapter 2 deals with self-observation. For me this chapter is very much interesting, I've made a lot of research while writing this chapter which talks about how to manage your time properly. Though this chapter is very small I find it interesting. The next three chapters explain practicing hard and preparing for success. Chapter 6 is all about pills and potions which means the medications for your wounds that make you stronger than ever. In this chapter, I've made some questionnaires for your self-analyzation and also gave solutions for your answers. Chapter 7 deals with the purpose of an internal motivation within you which discusses how to accomplish your dreams and transform them into your goals. Last but not least, the 8th chapter is a concluding one which makes me feel very satisfied because I've compiled the entire message conveyed in this book. I have tried my best to make the book free of errors. I apologize if any error is found. Please feel free to contact me through my email and reflect your comments to improve this book in upcoming editions. I sincerely thank my school Principal, Mr. Gopalakrishnan who encourages my writing since my school days till now. I cordially thank him for the time he spent reading and writing a foreword for this book.

Muthu pavithra,
pavithira.sarathy@gmail.com

ACKNOWLEDGEMENTS

"In-between tomorrow's dream and yesterday's regret is today's opportunity. Seize the chance

- Ifeanyi Enoch onuoha"

The book you are holding in your hand is a great dream in my life. This is a self-help book which could be read by the six sixties. My journey of writing this book does not have been possible without my family, friends, and well-wishers, especially my father **Mr. G.Parthasarathy,** without his support to publish my book this couldn't be in your hands. I thank this universe for making my dream come true. This book will help you to achieve your goals and dreams positively. Nothing comes out of hard work and struggle, I've worked day and night to make it a perfect one. I hope this book will impress you. I thank **Miss. Kamalipriya Karthik** for her illustrations in this book. Many people helped and motivated me during my writing journey. The main credit goes to author **Mr. S.Satheesh Kumar** who helped me in editing this book, without his patience and hard work it is impossible to complete my book. I've connected the contents with lots of stories and questionnaires which makes this book much more interesting. This book consists of eight chapters that will help you to achieve great heights in your life and will guide you whenever you feel low. In the following pages, I didn't write anything new. I just reminded you of something that you missed somewhere in your life. I swear when you complete this book you will start to sketch the plans for your success.

I've learned a lot during this journey of writing, which made me correct and understand myself. This was my first book, I don't want this book to be a bestseller. If one reader gets motivated and succeeded by reading my work that completely marks the success of my book. That's what I want.

MuthuPavithra G.P.

I

Plan and Pursue it

Does it make any sense to plan before you do something? Anyhow you are not going to follow the plans you made, then what is the purpose of making plans? Are you the person who plans something and not getting better results? I'm sure that you are not the only one who perfectly plans for nothing; we all are the different feathered birds under the same sky. Joke's apart Get quiet and be honest with yourself, if you are not correctly aligned with your schedule then it is relevant that you are chasing the wind and you know about the results.

> "***A good plan is like a road map: it shows the final destination and usually the best way to get there***
>
> *- H. Stanley Judd.*"

What do you do when you plan?

- You will create a new design for your plan.

- You hang that schedule on your wall where there are already many schedules you have hung.
- On the first day of your schedule, you feel better about your plans.
- But after a week or a month you feel bored and you skip to your next plan. This is where you fail.
- The next problem is when you start to plan for work, you are also planning for the results, there where you get confused about what you were supposed to do?
- The priority of the plan is not about the results, it's actually about the action taken towards your achievement, and not deciding about what you will be achieving.
- You will be influencing your mind to focus only on the results, and not on the work you want to complete because you need your schedule to be comfortable, there is where you are injecting a slow poison towards your ability.
- You will make some time limits in your schedule which is going to result in nothing; you will continue with those timings and you won't even bother to follow through because you don't care enough.
- You will work for 20 minutes, and take a ten-minute break as per the schedule, which is a great joke.
- You will never be allowed to work more than a minute from your scheduled time.
- Finally, you feel bad for not getting better results.

> ***"A good plan implemented today is better than a perfect plan implemented tomorrow!"***
>
> *- George Patton.*

What should you want to do when you plan?

- Analyze your previous plans and identify where things went wrong that leads to failure. And correct it.
- Do not make a monthly schedule; just plan for a week at first. The journey is more important than your destination.
- Don't plan just for your work; it leads to stress. Enhance your mind and body to be relaxed. Start controlling your senses through meditation.
- Do not make a plan with your diary or white paper; create a calendar for yourself. You should sketch in all of your work, additional events, and so on.
- Once all of these are plotted in your calendar, you will be able to make clear your plans. Stick to your plans, which means that if you adopt these habits daily, this will be a powerful weapon to keep you on your way to reaching your destiny. Confucius says **"It does not matter how slowly you go, as long as you do not stop."**
- Plan for short breaks.

Plan for success

A plan will help you to establish and organize your ideas. Planning is the only key to achieving your goals. Don't fix your mind stick to laziness, because once you skip something for a day it makes you stressed out about upcoming work; this is the only reason for rescheduling. Mindset is everything, an optimistic mindset will change your entire life. Don't allow your mind to think negatively, once your views and thoughts about your work become negative, then there is no use of plenty of hard work day and night, keep your thoughts positive. Though you can't complete your work on time, your positivity can manage you and it helps you to be energetic at your work. You should know that you are worthy of anything you desire. Being successful doesn't mean only success; it comes to you by taking risks. Your success depends on your plan; whether your plan is short-term or long-term; you must plan accordingly to achieve your goal. Short-term plans should be completed daily and are easier to achieve your destiny. Long-term plans are also known as strategic plans based on a long-range vision. Both plans help you achieve your goals. I've heard a story about planning which motivates me to achieve my targets on time. Once Confucius was passing by a village, where he saw an old man with his young son taking water from the well. Confucius was confused to see this, as at that time people harnessed horses or oxen to pull water from the well. Confucius with concern went to the old man and said, "why are you necessarily tiring yourself and the young man, that now we have harnessed horses and oxen...?" The old man hushed him and said "please speak softly. I don't want my son to hear this...! I can answer you, but please come back when my son goes for lunch," said the old man. Confucius was perplexed.

He kept quiet and waited until the old man came to him alone at lunchtime. Confucius questioned, "why would you not let your son hear what I said?" the old man replied, "I am 85 years old and yet I have the strength to work side by side 30 years old, young. If today I engage horses to pull the water, then my son will not be able to have the same strength at 85, that I have now. That's why I asked you not to speak about it in front of my son. It's a question of his health. We heard that townspeople use horses to pull water from wells. There are machines also to do that. But if I use horses or machines now, then what will he do? What effect will it have on my son's health?" Said the old man. The moral of this story is that what we do today will affect us tomorrow. What we do on the one hand has an immediate effect on the other. He who rests in the day destroys his response of the night. So, plan wisely according to your visions. These planning strategies are just a learning process to achieve your destiny. Have you ever forgotten to charge your phone once a day, no right; likewise you should charge your habits like laziness, procrastination, running from your problems, turning on distractions, because these are the only reasons for your success being delayed!

What success demands you?

Your sacrifices mean your success. Success is not something to learn from others. It is the learning process of one's own learning and experiences. You have to create your pathway to reach your destination. Sacrifices don't mean losing your potential; you should leave all the happiness for your success. Without sacrificing something, you can't achieve anything in your life. Also, hardworking through sacrifices doesn't mean you skip your food, miss a meetup with friends and family, or do laborious work or the work that makes you sweat. Hard work is something like a healthy body with a sound mind to be a successful person. Your willpower and your positive attitude towards your decisions are the keys to your success. So be attentive to your body and soul.

Tips to be a successful person

- Don't limit your schedule.
- Develop positive habits.
- Improve your skills, Keep learning.
- Be a person who is capable of thinking critically and making bold decisions to reach your desired goals.
- Try to picture your goals and dreams, so that you can work more than before.
- Don't think about yourself as a loser; you are not a failure unless you stop trying.
- Also, don't miss the fun part of your journey so have fun along the way, but don't lose your perspective.
- Be honest with your work and yourself, because you are the only person who manages all your plans and identifies solutions for your problems to push yourself towards success.

- Don't allow your mind to get into distractions because they kill your sacrifices, hard work, time, and energy.
- Assign tasks to yourself according to your calendar, so that you can always stick to your mistakes and make improvements in your progress.
- Learn to balance your time and work.
- Don't worry about failures, because failure is simply the opportunity to begin again, this time more intelligently.
- Never give up, because when you give up you are judging yourself as a loser. So, believe in your ability.
- Be a person of action; do wait for the correct time to execute your work.
- None of us succeeds immediately, so wait for some time to achieve our goals, automatically your energy sums up what you can do with your time.

There is no success without failure

Your success or failure don't define who you are; only your hard work and sacrifices define your success. Without losing your enthusiasm, you just keep on moving towards your destiny of success. Walt Disney says, ***"All our dreams can come true if we dare to pursue them"*** which is obvious that we should be able to pursue our dreams of success with courage. Learn from your failures because there are so many people who are succeeded after so many failures. Do you know, *Chaplin's* first character in a film was not a success and critics said he looked too young. So, the 24-year-old added mustache and baggy trousers, transforming into the tramp which would make him a star. There are no definitions and structures for your success. Many successful people once had been unknown persons. The only thing they all said is never, ever give up. Oliver and Wilbur Wright, these brothers battled depression and family illness before starting the bicycle shop that would lead them to experiment with flight. After numerous attempts at creating flying machines, several years of hard work, and tons of failed prototypes, the brothers finally created a plane that could get airborne and stay there. So, as we all say, failures are the steps for success. Never demotivate yourself after facing a failure. Zig Ziglar says, ***"Remember that failure is an event, not a person".*** A failure is not always a fault, it is more important to heed the lessons of failure. Every mistake of one's own experience can feed him something to his success. Be grateful for your failures, and keep your vision towards success.

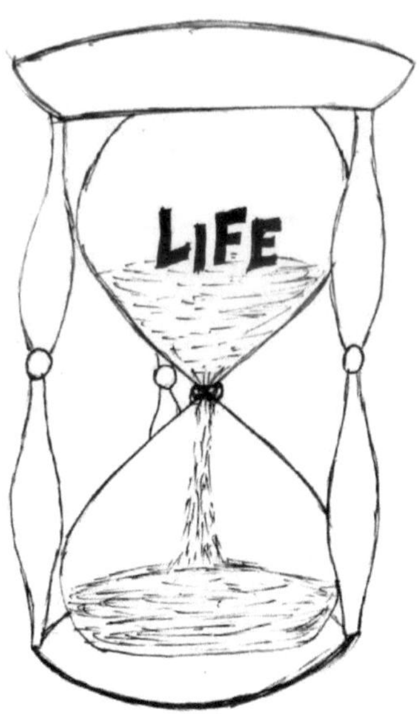

Plan to Manage your time effectively

You can lead a healthy and happy life if you have learned how to make use of your own time. It may be tricky, but it is somewhat easy when you find out what tricks you to manage your time. Good time management gives you a stress-less completion of your work. Managing your time without any impediments will lead to more opportunities. Now let's look at some ways to manage time effectively.

- **Give an early start to your day.**
- **Be clear with your ambition.**
- **Find out where you are wasting your time most.**
- **Focus on your tasks**
- **Prioritize tasks based on importance and urgency.**
- **Set a time limit.**
- **Avoid distractions.**
- **Take short breaks between tasks.**
- **Make a stop-doing list.**
- **Know your deadlines, and decide prior.**
- **Have a mini-plan for the day.**

What happens when you fail to manage your time?

- You feel like you are procrastinating most of your planned work, and you are not able to complete your tasks on time.
- You have done nothing in a day to attain your goals than simply consume your energy and time.

- You often go on missing your deadlines, which leads to major problems.
- You will suffer from depression and stress due to incompliance with your work.
- You feel very low, and that leads you to think in a negative direction.
- Not being able to schedule your tasks effectively.
- Failing to manage your distractions.
- Multitasking leads to a workload.
- As much as we project ourselves as a busier person differs from being an effective person, we sometimes lose our paths and travel in the wrong direction, and find ourselves doing low-priority work that completely erupts our energy and time, to avoid this scenario, ask yourself

1. What I'm doing will help me to reach my destiny?
2. Could it be possible to make me a successful person?
3. How does this lead to the ultimate goal?
4. What are the things to be listed to reach my goal?
5. What are my to-do's?

Goal setting is nothing but a destination where you want to be 5 or 10 years from now. the destination is something that you have chosen to be traveled (going) to reach your goal. To reach your destination at the correct time you have to make a master plan as mentioned above. Remember " ***A goal without a plan is just a wish***". Make sure to fit in where ever you are to attain your goals

II

Self-Observation

The only way to reach your destiny is to keep yourself aware of your time and energy which makes you successful. Once you know where you lag you can use your schedule and strategies to manage your time. monitoring your progress is a slow process of success. You can easily monitor your progress in progress towards your destiny by managing your time effectively.

- Maintain a daily task long for 3-7 days.
- From the time you wake up till the time you go to bed, analyze the activities you have done, notice the time you have started and finished, and record the amount of time each task consumed.
- Focus on the completion of one task at a time
- Increase your confidence by reducing your stress levels.
- Getting plenty of sleep, receiving around 8 hours of sleep every night is essential to an effective mind, and it allows you to be more productive.
- At the end of each day, analyze yourself with these questions,

1. what tasks have I done high, medium, or low?
2. Am I happy with the way I use my time?
3. Am I wasting my time on any least productive activities?
4. Am I focusing on, what was most important to me?
5. Where can I save some time?
6. Is there anything I need to change?

- Once you find where you are lagging, and how your time is being wasted, you can manage your time effectively without any hurdles.

How does time affect your life?

People used to say that the most valuable commodity you have is time; use it wisely. Don't multitask to save your time; instead concentrate on one thing at a time, to the fullest. Time was unique, it is the most important thing in human life. The only thing that you can't buy with money is time. Successful people always think that time is an opportunity to improve themselves. Once upon a time, a very strong woodcutter asked for a job from a timber merchant, and he got it. The wages for his work were really good as he expected, and so were the work conditions. For those reasons, the woodcutter was determined to do justice. His boss gave him an ax and showed him the area where he was supposed to work. On the first day, the woodcutter brought 18 trees. "Congratulations, you have done a great job," the boss said. "carry on!" the woodcutter was very much motivated by his words, the woodcutter worked harder the very next day, but he could only bring 14 trees. On the third day, he tried even harder, but he could only bring 9 trees. Day after day he was bringing fewer and fewer trees and it goes on days passed. " I must be losing my energy and so I couldn't make any progress", the woodcutter thought. He went to the boss and apologized, saying that he could not understand what was going on. "When was the last time you sharpened your ax?" the boss asked. "Sharpen? The woodcutter went silent for a minute and replied, I had no time to sharpen my ax. I have been very busy trying to cut trees..." Imagine this for a second— the "trees" in this short story represent your goals and the "ax" represents 'you'. What can we learn from this? The secret of high progress leads to not managing the time properly or hard work—it's all about engaging yourself, especially your potential. We all have the same 24 hours every day but then why do some people achieve more in their lives, it's not because of managing their time better, it's because they manage their lives and energy better. Life and time are the two best chapters to be learned about how to make good use of time and to nourish the value of our life.

Break up with your phone

I hope this title irritates you. The reality is your phone is one of the slow poisons that you take in your mind daily. The reason for your plans getting delayed is your addiction to mobile phones. I'm not requesting you to fully cut off from your phone, but you can help you to break free of the addiction and balance your activities to lead a happy and healthy life. Our phones are designed to addict us. You are thinking that your day starts with your alarm and ends with setting up an alarm. But according to me your day starts and ends with your smartphone. It's not bad to use phones, but it's really bad to get addicted to the internet world and smartphones. *Aziz Ansari* says, ***"whenever you check for a new post on Instagram or whenever you go on the New York times to see if there's a new thing, it's not even about the content. It's just about seeing a new thing. You get addicted to that feeling"*** why are you addicted to smartphones? Have you ever questioned yourself? Let me know! Smartphones are unique from other technologies. They are unique in a lot of good ways, also there are a lot of disadvantages, they disturb us while we are working, they always grab our attention towards them, it makes us think with a smartphone we are nothing. Am I correct? Most of these technologies involve a brain chemical called Dopamine. Dopamine is a chemical messenger. It affects many parts of your behavior and physical functions. Dopamine plays many roles. But for our purposes dopamine makes us feel excited and happy. Dopamine makes us feel excited every time, and we like to be excited right! Anything we experience that triggers the release of dopamine is that wants you to experience it again and again. If your brain learns to check your phone regularly, you are addicted to it. Research has shown that people who overuse cell phones may experience

- Anxiety
- Depression
- Sleep deficits
- Relationship conflicts
- Poor academic or work performance.

Researchers believe that people who compulsory use cell phones may try to avoid issues in their lives that feel complicated. How many times do you check your phone each day? 25 times. That isn't even close to reality. Apple Says that "iPhone users unlock their phones 80 times a day" think about yours. When are you going to give independence for your mind from this digital drug addiction? We are allowing our minds on a battlefield our minds are at war and we have willingly subjected ourselves to digital devices. So let's stop getting addicted ourselves to this digital world and let us give independence for our minds from today.

III

Practice beyond necessities

You are the only responsible person for your own life. Practice can make everything possible; one must know the importance of practice; it is the reputation of your actions. It is an activity that repeats regularly. You must be aware of what you are going to do with your plans for the future. Your tasks never end until you complete them. What I am saying is to Practice what makes you perfect. Practice boosts your energy. It just pushes us up to work harder and harder to reach our goals successfully. Regular activities improve your quality of life, try to practice your best. Practice is not a direct path for your success. It's just an improvement that leads to success. Daily practice makes you a perfectionist. Once there lived a young girl in Japan whose dream was to become a singer. Singing was her passion and that's what she always wanted to do. She got a very disciplined mentor. He asked the girl to practice on a particular song over and over again, every day for months. The girl got exasperated and she ran away in the thought of giving up on singing. One day she went to a restaurant for dinner, where a singing competition was going. The host asked anyone from the public willingly to sing a song of their choice.

The girl agreed and sang the one song that she practiced regularly. Her performance was outstanding and the judges judged her and asked who her instructor was? Then the girl realized that her instructor had been a true mentor, by making her practice the same thing again and again to achieve perfection. The girl was popularly known as Japanese singer Fubuki Koshiji. We all are interested in learning something, but we are not interested in learning them regularly, which leads to failure. All of us have experienced one thing during our school days that are particularly during our examinations. After getting the question paper, we will check for the questions that are well known. But the thing is at least there will be three or four questions in our question paper that we studied but can't answer it only because of not practicing well and we will sit there and think oh! Gosh, I've studied this but I should have practiced well it's all my mistakes. There is no use in thinking about the action that makes no sense right. Do something to make sure you are becoming the best version of yourself. You are exactly what you practice every day. To practice something endlessly, what should you follow?

Analyze your fears and accomplish your goals

Have you ever asked yourself about your fears? What scares you while thinking about practicing something? What makes you not want to come out of your comfort zone? Our lives today are controlled by fears. I'm sure you have had an experience with it in the past. Once I've read a story about the fear of elephants which helped me to come out from my fears and I wish you too! As a man was passing the elephants, he suddenly stopped, confused by the fact that these huge creatures were being held by only a small rope tied to their front leg. No chains, no cages. It was obvious that the elephants could, at any time, break away from their bonds but for some reason, they did not. He saw an elephant trainer nearby and he asked why these animals just stood there and made no attempt to getaway. The trainer said, *"when they are very young and much smaller, we use the same size rope to tie them and, at that age, it's enough to hold them. As they grow up, they are conditioned to believe they cannot break away. They believe the rope can still hold them, so they never try to break free."* The man was amazed, these animals could at any time break free from their bonds but because they believed they couldn't, they were stuck right where they were. Like elephants, we are also convincing our minds to believe that we can't do something, simply because we failed at it once before. Fears arise from the belief we have in something. I'm just saying break the chains, don't allow your fears to control you. Free up your mind. Fear holds you back from achieving your success. We always have a nasty habit of interrupting the best-laid plans, but what makes us the fear of achieving something without any practice? When you are triggered by an unpleasant perception of danger that is either real or imaginary, you feel this primitive emotion called fear. Your fears destroy your goals. In every aspect, achieving your goal is very difficult. Goals should be challenging, they should push you, help to make you a better person. Goals should pull you away from your comfort zone. Your fear completely erupts your energy and destroys your plans. There are many things to do in your life. Don't allow your fears to pull down your success. If you are afraid of the consequences of your actions. You won't able to achieve your success and you'll stand halfway. There are many strategies to overcome your fears. You should overcome your fear by imagining the worst things that you have faced with a strong determination. Because when you recollect the worst face of your life you can easily boost up your mind and overcome fears by answering yourself this too can pass away. Don't allow yourself to believe something which is not true. Robin Sharma says ***"The fears we don't face becomes our limits."*** You have to conquer your fears to achieve your goals by

- Develop your confidence
- Master your motivation
- Built leadership confidence within you.

Take extra responsibility

You should be a responsible person for the plans you have made. So that you can achieve your destiny without any hurdles. Being Responsible arises from the purpose to complete something much needed on time Being a responsible person is one of good quality and requires planning. Planning plays a major role in being a responsible personality. A King had four daughters, he wanted to see what the responsibilities he can give to them. So, he gave some wheat grains to each one of them and asked them to come back after a year. After a year he called all the four daughters and inquired about the wheat.

First daughter: On the same day I fed it to sparrows thinking that they were meant for that. King did not give any responsibility to her.

you can't escape from your responsibilities.

Second daughter: I mixed them in the Bhandara thinking that they are sacred and so that everyone could have them.

King: OK you take care of Bhandara.

Third daughter: I saved them safely along with my jewelry and here they are.

King: OK you take care of the treasury

Fourth daughter: I need two bullocks and two men to get the wheat. All of them laughed and asked why? she said, "I sowed the grains and now it's grown so big that I need to harvest it and get it on carts.

King: Good, you are the best. You take care of the whole house and he gave her the keys. This story simply explains how responsibilities made your efforts to become a successful person. Your responsibilities shaped you into a better person. Utilize your abilities to attempt your tasks and accomplish your goals.

If you are good at planning then be perfect in practice

There is a famous quote, ***"practice makes a man perfect"*** but reality manifests something unexpected, like practice alone, cannot make you a perfectionist. You should have some good features within you. Planning something is always a pleasure to work with. But you should always be aware of what you plan? And how do you practice? Planning is not a big commitment but practicing something new is a little difficult. Many of us excuse ourselves for our mistakes and deflect responsibility for the situation.

Practice makes you a confident person and confidence within you creates motivation and being sure with your abilities. Believe in yourself and your ability, don't care about what others think about your life. Ask yourself! What is possible? If you try hard to achieve destiny without giving up, everything will be possible. So never lose hope!

Don't be afraid of challenges

I believe the quote saying, "fear is the killer of your dreams" fear can forbid us to achieve our destiny. Adopt the changes and accept the challenges around you. Most of us don't fear challenges, we are all afraid of the results of those challenges. If you are worried about your failures, then you can't reach your success forever. It's almost impossible to go through life without experiencing some kind of failure. If you are leading a life without any failures, I swear you have never seen any success in your life. Failure makes you believe that you are helpless, but a lot of people find things easier and highly beneficial to think out of sense. Many successful people have come across many failures in their lives,

Michael Jordan

Michael Jordan is widely considered one of the greatest basketball players of all time. Yet he says, I've missed more than 9,000 shots in my career," ***I've lost 300 games, twenty-six times I've trusted to take the game-winning game shot and missed. I've failed over and over and over again in my life and that is why I succeeded".***

Charles Darwin

Darwin is considered as one of the most influential scientists about theories on natural selection and evolution have had a major impact on our understanding of species and life here on earth, along with the progress of biological organisms. Darwin dropped out of medical school. In his autobiography, Darwin knew that others including his father were displeased with him. He stated, ***"I was considered by all my master's and my father, as a very ordinary boy, rather below the common standard of intellect."*** He was summed up as a failure throughout his life. Of course, things don't remain the same in his life.

Chris Gardener

The most inspiring movie in the present day among all of us, The pursuit of happiness, starring will smith, got released in 2006 which was a Gardener's autobiography, about his early failures and struggles in his life. If you have seen the movie, you already know how it happened. Gardener struggled a lot throughout his life. But he never gave up and he was committed to leading a better life. But during the journey of his life, he suffered through rejections, homelessness, jail, and eventual divorce. But those struggles he faced don't stop him from overcoming his failures.

Emily Dickinson

Dickinson considered herself a failure for much of her life. Being an introvert, she was reluctant to embrace face-to-face relationships. Dickinson became one of the most renowned poets in history. Less than a dozen of poems were published during her lifetime. While Dickinson believed in herself as a failure during her lifetime. It was only due to her reluctance to meet people. However, after her death, her sister discovered her poems and helped her to gain international notoriety and fame.

The Beatles

The Beatles were an English rock group that was formed in 1960. They have since gone on to sell over 1.6 billion records worldwide. The Beatles were considered one of the most popular musical groups in history. Its members were John Lennon, George Harrison, Paul Mc Cartney, and Ringo Starr. However, they have once considered themselves as a failure. They had faced many rejections but they didn't give up which made them famous worldwide. So don't be afraid of challenges and facing failures, because success needs lots of challenges and failures in our life. Life instructs you to go on sometimes when you face failures, which helps you in learning about yourself. Don't allow your mind to believe something that you don't deserve.

Keep learning

Angelina Jolie says, ***"without pain, there would be no suffering, without suffering we would never learn from our mistakes. To make it right, pain and suffering are the keys to all windows without it there is no way of life."*** Learning is a one-way practice that will help you to identify who you are? What is the purpose of your action? And how do you pursue your dreams? Have you ever gotten bored, roaming here and there inside your house and doing nothing? If so, how come you will spend your time. Learning something new and exciting! People who learn a lot will get better. In his famous 2005 Commencement speech for Stanford University, Jobs said: ***"If I had never dropped in on that single calligraphy course in college, the Mac would have never had multiple typefaces or proportionally spaced fonts."*** during the journey of your learning, you should never forget to concrete yourself.

IV

The miracle power of yourself

There is a lot of difference between your inner self and outer self. You can't show up every behavior in front of everyone. But you know who you are? And how much do you know about yourself? You can learn a lot by yourself. Focus on your thoughts and give some time to creativity and it's obvious that you are unique from others so you don't want to worry about others' opinions expressed upon you. Fit your mind into deep meditation and exercise your body regularly. You can improve yourself by learning something new every day. Don't allow your mind to think in a negative perception, life couldn't be more surprising if you have done everything perfectly, so balance both pros and cons of your actions and decisions equally.

Apparent sources

This is what, most of us follow in our day-to-day lives. You could have experienced a lot of people in your daily life and you could have learned a lot from them. People like parents, teachers, and mentors are the only personalities who played a major role in our lives. And they have been a great support to learn many unknown sources. When you start to accept yourself with others' perceptions, you feel better about your abilities and skills. Humans are the creatures of learning, it's the best practice to improve ourselves day by day from birth till our death, which makes the world a better place. Focus on making things better not big!

Experience makes you nonpareil

You learn something if you fail to achieve your goals. You never learn after achieving your goals. Because according to you the achievements you have concocted are enough for you. But reality vacillates from your thoughts and opinions. If you have achieved something, this world expects a spare. If you botched others' expectations, then instinctively you will be forgotten. Experience is the best weapon that sharpens your failures and helps you to rectify your mistakes. Every day is an opportunity to make sense of your learning process. Ask yourself at the end of the day... "what are the experiences I've learned today?" Whatever, I'll try to learn something good from my experience!" Getting hold of new skills and consuming information of knowledge on a daily incremental basis is a proven way too vigilant for your self-esteem.

Allow your inner self to guide

Sometimes your comfort zone and confidence level need to be challenged. There are times when you must take a few extra opportunities and create your reality. You must be capable of changing your priorities according to your situation and rearranging yourself to reach your destiny. You should always appreciate yourself for taking up the opportunities to grow, develop and you should always be aware of finding the true sense of purpose of your own life. Be confident enough to achieve your goals and objectives.

Cultivate your plans and practice them hard

Your progress is not about what you plan, it is based on what you practice and how you qualify yourself with your abilities! I assure you that you are the only perfect person in the world and I just want you to believe what I said, do you agree? If you agreed with my statement, then you started to think that you are unique from others who are perfect. Likewise, you should invariably Cognition about your plans. *Billie Jean King* says, ***"I'll keep playing until they get it right"*** you can win anything if you practice it hard. Suddenly you can't practice something endlessly, you should start practicing first. Captivate your plans and ideas and practice what makes you perfect and you can easily boost up your better version. Karoly Takacs lost his main shooting hand in a grenade explosion. A year later, after disappearing for months, he came back as a champion shooter with his left hand. But it took him another 9 years to win the gold medal. The previous champion congratulated Takacs by jokingly saying he had learned enough. Takacs went on to win the gold medal in the same event in the 1952 Olympics too... A normal person with a dream of becoming the best shooter in the world would simply give up. But Karoly did not do. He had one dream and one dream only. "To have the best shooting hand in the world." He learned to shoot with his left hand and practiced so much that he went on to win Olympics gold medals. Twice. His never-ending effort for the piece of metal earned him a place on the list of Olympic heroes. Henry Ford says, ***"whether you think you can, or cannot be right"*** your body believes what your subconscious mind says. Wait for your victory until you get it. Keep practicing until you live your own experience of your life.

V

Preparation is the major desire

There is an old dictum that claims, ***"It is better to be safe than sorry."*** Most of us agree with this statement. One should be better prepared before executing something. The leverage of preparation is that you can manage your dilemma quickly and you will undoubtedly find solutions for your obstacles. Preparation is a learning skill that can improve your experience with your abilities. Jim Rohn says, ***"To give it and to share it, and for it to be effective, you first need to have it. Good communication starts with good preparation. A Part of success is preparation on purpose."*** Preparation is vital for people from all walks of life. Going through life without preparation is like building without a blueprint. inform yourself with your great efforts and preparation day by day. Once upon a time, After he had studied Zen for ten years, a monk attained the rank of Zen teacher. And one rainy day soon after his advancement, he journeyed to visit his old zen master. When he walked into the house the master greeted him with a question. "Tell me, did you leave your sandals and umbrella on the porch?" yes" replied the teacher. And tell me, did you leave your umbrella to the left or the right of your sandals? The teacher realized he did not know the answer, and that he had not yet attained full awareness. He stayed and studied with the master for ten more years. What does this story preach to you...Is in your life "it is not important that how much time you spent preparing something, the importance lies within how much of yourself you put into that preparation"

Benefits of being prepared

Confucius says, ***"Success depends upon previous preparation, and without such preparation, there is sure to be a failure."*** Preparation is an essential accessory to make your life meaningful. We all are once being failing somewhere, but have you ever questioned yourself why you are prepared to attempt it? Yes! Don't blink, you are the only person who is prepared for your success or failure. Once you didn't try something after your failures, I swore that you have never thought about the benefits of being prepared for anything, the truth is, you can plan all you want, but if you don't prepare, you still won't be ready.

Is there any difference between planning and preparation?

"Planning insists you be aware. Preparation insists you be ready" Preparation is also important as like planning. When it comes to planning you have already scheduled a "to-do list" and you can easily boost up your mind to get into what you have planned, but planning alone cannot help you to achieve your goals. The problem is that we can create a plan, but you will easily get distracted by the pessimism around you. So, you have to be prepared. Being prepared is nothing but the creation of additional plans. If you failed with your Plan-A, then move with Plan- B. The plan to bring prepared is to examine the alternatives. Be aware of what you plan to master in your preparation. Preparation is an added part of your planning strategies. Both depend upon each other.

How to be prepared?

Proper preparation prevents poor performance. A huge part of your daily deals with managing your stress, unpreparedness, frustration, and so on. The main part is how this stuff arises, and how you react to it. There are a few tips to follow that leave your path to preparation.

Understand what you have been doing

Albert Einstein says, ***"Any fool can know the point is to understand."*** The warning that your mind needs every minute is the learning process from every mistake. If you understand your mistakes better, you can easily understand what you have to prepare for next. And you will come to realize that everything that you need is within you. Have you ever recollected what you have been doing the last time when you prepared, and what you have gained and what you have lost? If no is your answer, then question yourself about your preparation for success. You can avoid those last-minute disasters when you prepared properly.

Complete in advance

Since we can't understand what are preparations will be most needed in advance, then it will become senseless to learn something for the future. If you are prepared to complete your work prior, then you will have enough time to stick with unanticipated exertion. You should always be ready to face the challenge in advance. Preparation is all about executing and contemplating, your thinking process in advance. When you started to complete your work in advance you can make yourself unruffled. Abraham Lincoln says, ***"Give me six hours to chop down a tree and I will spend the first four sharpening the ax."*** so if you make your priorities limpid, you can easily evaluate your endeavors.

VI

Pills and potions

You could have blamed yourself for the mistakes you have made in the past. But have you ever examined why you did this? Your mindset on all your problems is one of the best weapons to manage your attitude in a good way. I'm not insisting on you being happy and chill all the time. But whenever your anxiety level is very high, just think and act because you can't Collect the pennies once you spend. It is very important to think ahead before any instinctive actions you make.

Master your stress

Hush... I'm stressed. We all used to say this once a day, but the reality is we are not stressed, but we believe that stress is something triggered by the events involved in our life. William James says, "The greatest weapon against stress is our ability to choose one thought over another". Once there lived a great writer named Stanley, whose age was around fifty. One day he decided to go out for a walk; he couldn't even stand up from his sofa. So he decided to take some rest. A few minutes later he feels pain in the upper part of his body. so, he thought of calling his friend Charles, who is a doctor, to check on him. He is older than Stanley. When Charles reached Stanford apartments, where his friend Stanley lives on the third floor, he felt very tired to climb the steps. Somehow, once, he reached the third floor. He Searched for a sofa after entering the foyer(hall). Hey Charles, you are aged up man, said Stanley and they both had some funny conversations among them. Then he decided to bring some coffee for Charles, and he made a cup of coffee and served him. Charles asked him in a doubtable tone, "Stanley, you said you are unhealthy, but then you are serving coffee for me" Stanley replied that it's a manner to serve our guests. Then Charles had a coffee and started his treatment for Stanley. Charles asked questions about his health, like " what makes him feel unhealthy and where does he feel pain" he said the upper part of his body is paining. Charles laughs and said, No it doesn't pain for you, think and tell where it is paining. Then after a minute, he said his right hand is aching, Charles seriously said, no it is not paining for you Stanley, I think you are perfect. Then he said my wrist is paining Charles, I can't write anything and it makes me feel very low. After a few minutes, Charles gave some medicine for his wrist pain. And he advised him to take a rest for a week. Then Charles left his house. Could you guess the ethics of this story? Stanley lives in me and you. We believe that we are stressed and we are cheating ourselves. We are just repeatedly thinking about stress, and not analyzing why we are stressed and how should we come out from this? Have you ever thought of any solutions, more than thinking about your problem? When you think too much about something, you don't get any idea to solve it. Just stop imagine about your problems, then you feel easy to handle your stress.

Does it important to master your stress Have you ever questioned yourself? It is really important to master your stress during the journey of understanding yourself. Ok now let's have some questionnaires about stress...

1. <u>**What are the main causes of your depression?**</u>

A)It happens because of my situation

- Does it last for a moment or longer time?
- Can you understand what leads you to this situation.?
- Are you feeling unhappy and unprepared for your situation?
- Have you tried to come out from this?
- Are you ready to face your situation?
- In what perspective you are approaching your situation?
- What is the support you can gain to come out from this situation?
- How you are preparing yourself to come out from this?
- What are the transformations you need to handle this situation?
- What is this situation trying to teach you?

B)Bullying

- According to you, what is bullying?
- What type of bullying do you face, among these?

1. Physical bullying.
2. Verbal bullying.
3. Psychological bullying.
4. Cyberbullying.

- Are you suffering from any mental and physical trauma?
- Have you ever felt like losing your confidence while getting bullied, either temporarily or permanently?

- Do you think, someone can help you to cope with bullying?
- Do you know about anti-bullying laws?
- Have you ever shared your feelings with someone about getting bullied?
- Are you an innocent person?
- Have you ever thought of avoiding getting into the traps of bullies?
- Can you stop getting bullied? if yes what are steps you have taken to avoid this?
- Where do you get bullied?

1. At the workplace
2. At school
3. At college
4. At family

C) Serious illness

- What leads you to this illness?
- Are you taking medications?
- What is the ailment you are suffering from?
- What is the prevention you have done to save yourself?
- Are you worried about your future?
- What are the support systems you have chosen, that are right for your health?
- Do you get enough sleep and maintain the correct time to eat?
- What is your hobby?
- Do you think your illness is a drawback for your ambitions?
- What do you listen to the most to change your thoughts about your illness?

- Does your illness affect you emotionally?

D) Other Personal Problems

- Are you able to share your problems with others?
- Does it relate to a health crisis or money crisis?
- Are you confused?
- Do you share your problems with friends and family?
- Are you a thinker?
- Are you the person who stays in the past?

2. Have you ever questioned yourself about your failures?

A) I am not a person who is anxious about failures.

- Do you believe strongly that failure is the stepping stone to success?
- What are the kinds of stuff you have learned from your failures?
- What are your views on failure?

B) Yes, sometimes I feel like a loser.

- What made you feel that you are a loser?
- Have you ever been surrounded with motivation?
- Do you make excuses yourself?
- Do you value others' thoughts about you?
- According to you in what aspect you are a loser?
- Do you love yourself?
- Have you ever focused upon your strength?

C) I am frightened about other's view upon me

- What do you think about this society?
- Do you value yourself?
- Do you want to be in other good books?
- Do you take responsibility for your emotions?
- Does it matter what others think about you?

D) Failure is the only reason for my depression

- Have you ever thought of overcoming your failures?
- How do you cope with failures?
- Is it possible that you are not depressed, and you are using depression as an excuse for all your failures?

3. Have you ever usually stayed calm, even under a lot of pressure?

A) Yes

- Do you have the ability to control your emotions?
- How will you respond, when you are in a pressured situation?
- Why do you respond this way? Does responding in such a way hurts you?
- What do you want to gain in this situation?
- What are the benefits of staying calm?
- Do you get good quality of sleep?

B) No

- Do you practice meditation?
- Do you have plenty of sleep regularly?
- Do you think before you speak?
- Are you relaxed?
- Are you surrounded by positive thoughts?

Have you answered all these questions, do you find any solutions for your problems? If not, let me help you in finding a solution.

1. Main causes for your depression

You are the only person who is the reason for your situation, that you blame. There is nothing to lose when you are stressed because depression is a symptom of feeling sad and loss of interest.

A) It happens because of my situation

Situational depression is short-term stress that develops after you experienced a traumatic event. Past experiences in your life can affect the way you deal with stress. Your mistakes are the results of depression. And you can't blame the situation, because you deserve the strength of your effectiveness. When you blame your situation or other people you are maintaining a comfort zone around you, and you are expecting somebody to change your life. I'll tell you a short story about the blame game. If you feel unhappy about your problems, then train your mind to be happy, get prepared to reach your destiny. Everything you need is to change the situation you have to plan for coming out from this, focus on what you have, and accept the situation. Only by accepting, can let you go out of negative thinking. You can easily adapt to situations if you have control over your mental and physical health. Don't wait for opportunities, just create them, and let your actions pursue your dreams. There is a lot to learn from little mistakes, so correct your mistakes and be a philosopher for yourself. Leonardo DiCaprio says, "only you and you alone can change your situation. Don't try to blame it on anything or anyone". Focus on fixing the problems you have, don't search for reasons for blaming situations, you are the only responsible person for your problems.

B) Bullying

Bullying is a result of someone's perception. It can happen at any stage of life. It's an aggressive behavior of humans. Bullying is recognized by every society in the world. As we know there is always a difference and uniqueness between our origin, belief, culture, taste, caste, and birth. It's always a normal thing among human beings to dominate the stronger always dominates the weaker one. It is annoying behavior. There are many types of bullying. I want to share my experience with bullying. I am not the one who was surrounded by a circle of friends till my twelfth standard. I am not a top scorer in my school. The bullying I faced till my 10th standard was verbal bullying and psychological bullying. When I was at my tenth, I faced the situation of loneliness, inferiority complex, the taunt of gossip, and a name called the last bencher. The only friend I had till my twelfth was my mom who encourages me by saying, "If someone is teasing you and bullying you for what you are is not your fault, they are unlucky to have a friend like you, always believe you, one day your life will change as you wish. What I want to say is, when you are bullied by someone, just fix some target for you. And try to achieve those goals. Because life is what we wished to be. Bullying can happen in school, college, and the workplace. Sometimes even family members and parents are unknowingly involved in bullying. A UNESCO report says that 32% of students are bullied at schools worldwide. Bullying is becoming a major problem worldwide. There are many prevention strategies to overcome it. If you are bullied in your school, you can write a complaint letter to your teacher about your problem. And you should share it with your parents. If you are bullied at college, and in your workplace, there are certain laws to prevent it. You should compulsorily know about relevant sections of the Indian penal codes.

section 506 (punishment for criminal intimidation)

Criminal intimidation occurs when a person threatens another individual with injury to body, reputation, or property, criminal intimidation is also used by offenders to coerce students to not report this incident that has happened.

Section 323-326 (causing hurt and grievous hurt and the punishments for the same)

In cases resulting in the death of a victim of raging or bullying, this is self-explanatory. The actions of bullies cause hurt to the victim in certain cases.

Section 304 (the sections of IPC dealing with culpable homicide)

Culpable homicide is one of the most serious crimes under which a raging case can be booked. So don't be in a pressured state because of bullying. You can overcome it easily.

C) Serious illness

You have to listen to your doctor's advice and take certain medications. Don't overthink about the ailment you are suffering from, because it may Push up you in stress. You should take some preventions to secure yourself from your illness to save yourself. Don't worry about the future, because everything happens for a reason. Eat healthily, and be positive which can be a healing process for your mind and soul. Focus on your hobbies during your sickness. Don't think of your illness as a drawback for your ambitions because you are capable of anything you want. Positively change your attitude. In ancient times a king had his men place a huge rock on a roadway. He then hid in the bushes and watched if anyone would move the rock out of the way. Some of the king's wealthiest merchants and courtiers passed by and simply walked around it. Many people blamed the king for not keeping the roads clear. But none of them did anything about getting the stone removed. One day a peasant came along carrying vegetables upon approaching the rock. The peasant laid down his burden and tried to push the rock out of the way. After much pushing and straining, he finally managed. After the peasant went back to pick up his vegetables, he noticed a purse lying in the road where the rock had been. The purse contains many gold coins and a note from the king, explaining that the gold was for the person who removed the rock from the road. You see, in your life may be now you are suffering from a serious illness, but I'm sure definitely after all these obstacles allow you to improve your circumstances. You can create opportunities by fighting hard with your ill-health and you can do that by your generosity and willingness. So, try to make yourself comfortable to overcome your illness and see it as a chance to become better and to grow.

D) Other personal problems

Even though it is your personal, you should share it at least with your close friends or family. Get enough sleep, be as active as possible. Take care of yourself. Don't overthink your problems, which leads you to think in a negative direction. First of all, you should understand how you react to your problems? When you focus more on your problems, your mind gets upset and you tend to face many problems, if you focus on your possibilities you can create many opportunities. Once in a school, a teacher asked the students, " why Brake is placed in a car?" one student answered, " brake is used to reduce the speed of the car" Another student replied, " It is used to avoid accidents" then the other student told, " brake used to stop the car" another student told, " brake is used to ride a car very fast." The teacher asked him what you are saying that? Because brake's purpose is to stop the car right. The student replied, "if there is no break in the car, then we won't ride it fast, we only ride very slowly" the teacher praised him for his explanation. Like this, if there are no problems in our life, we can't improve ourselves. So don't worry about your problems, then you can't make your life better than your current version.

2. Have you ever questioned yourself about failures?

You can still wake up and fight for your success. Failure is nothing more than committing mistakes to achieve success. I am not a successful person in my life but I am always happy with my failures because I've learned many lessons from my failures, "experience failures more than success in your life because success doesn't teach you much but failures do".

A) I am not the person who is anxious about failures

You strongly believe that failure is the stepping stone to success, but you should always be aware of your mistakes to achieve success in your life. Jonny cash says, "I learn from my mistakes, it's a very painful way to learn, but without pain, the old saying is, there is no gain." you are not scared about failures. You can easily boost up your mind and you don't carry a lot of bitterness and anger, but you should always be aware of where you appreciate yourself and regret what you did? Because the most important part in our life during our failures are, the preparations and corrections towards success. You can't separate success from failure. Once upon a time, a person was coming to a new village relocating. And he was wondering if he would like it there. He went to a zen master and asked: "Do you think I will like it in this village? Are the people nice?" The master asked back, "how were the people in the town where you came from?" "They were nasty and greedy; they were angry and lived for cheating and stealing." "Those are exactly the type of people we have in this village", said the master. A day later, another newcomer to the village visited the master and asked the same question. To which the master asked, "how were the people in the town where you came from? "They were sweet and lived in harmony, they cared for one another...and for the land, they respected each other and they were seekers of spirits," he replied. "Well, those are exactly the type of people we have in this village.", said the master. If you are not anxious about failures, then it's like you are approaching your life with a positive attitude. If you always see the nasty part of your life, there is where you fail to see the good things within you. If you are the person who is not worrying about your failures, it means you are seeing good things within you. As Buddha says, "The mind is everything, what you think you become." So, think wisely and lead a happy and push yourself towards success.

B) Sometimes I feel like a loser

Your past experiences were the only reason for thinking of yourself as a loser. But there is no way to succeed without a past. Self-love is the best healing process to make yourself happy. Failure couldn't be the alternative to success. If you feel like a loser, it means that you don't learn lessons from your failures instead you have built a reputation for being a loser which makes no sense. Always be surrounded by positivity and positive people. Choose wisely and lead a happy life. Do you know that the most creative genius person of the twentieth century was once fired from the newspaper company for lack of creativity? Trying to persevere, Disney formed his first animation company, which was called Laugh-O-Gram Films. He raised $15,000 for the company but eventually was forced to close Laugh-O-Gram, following the close of an important distributor partner. Desperate and out of money, Disney found his way to Hollywood and faced even more criticism and failure until finally, his first few classic films started to skyrocket in popularity. Don't value others' thoughts upon you. Whatever you have lost is nothing, when you are charged up with my self-confidence and motivation. Focus only on your strength, which leads you to become a successful person.

C) I am frightened about others' view upon me

If you always value others' opinions upon you. Then you can't live peacefully, and you can't do what you like. When you value others' opinions, you started to live for others there is where you are getting caught by their opinions. Once upon a time, there lived a priest in a small village. He was a very innocent and simple-minded person, who minds his own business, and concentrated on performing religious rituals. On one occasion he was rewarded with a goat for his services by a wealthy man. The priest was happy to get a goat as a reward. He happily slung the goat over his shoulder and began the journey towards his home. On the way, three thugs saw the priest carrying the goat. All of them were lazy men, crooks, never wanted to work for their money. And so, they wanted to cheat the priest so that they could take away the goat. They said to themselves:

"This goat will make a delicious meal for all of us. Let's somehow get it." They discussed the matter amongst themselves and created a plan to get the goat by fooling the priest. After deciding on the plan, they separated from one another. And took different hiding positions at three different points on the way back to priests' homes. As soon as the priest arrived at one of the hiding places, one of the thugs came out and shockingly asked the priest: "sir, what are you doing? I don't understand why a holy man like you need to carry a dog on his shoulders?" the priest was surprised to hear such words, and he screamed: "can't you see it's not a dog you idiot, it's a goat!" The thug replied: "sir I beg your pardon, I told you what I saw. I'm sorry if you don't believe it. The priest was annoyed with the man and so he continued on his journey... while passing the second hideout, the second thug came out and asked the priest, "sir why are you carrying a dead calf on your shoulders?" you seem to be a wise person such an act is pure stupidity on your part" the priest yelled, "what? How can you mistake a living goat for a dead calf?" the second thug replied: "Sir, you seem to be highly mistaken in this regard, either you don't know what a goat looks like or you are doing it unknowingly. I just told you what I saw. Thank you and goodbye" the second thug walked around slightly smiling. The priest was confused, but he continued on his route. After a couple of minutes, he passed the third hideout. And the third thug came out, asking laughingly: "sir why do you carry a donkey on your shoulders? It makes you a laughing stock." Hearing the words of the third thug, the priest was worried, he started to think, "Is this not a goat, is this some kind of ghost?" he thought the animal he was carrying on his shoulders might be some sort of ghost because it transformed itself from a goat into a dog, from a dog to dead calf, from the dead calf into a donkey. The priest got frightened to such an extent that he hurled the goat on the roadside and ran away. The three thugs laughed at the priest, they caught the goat and were happy to enjoy the feast on it. Likewise, in your life don't get carried away by what others say, don't be fooled by those who want to take the good things from you, may it be positions or your energy. People may laugh at you and they may laugh at the things you have; they may laugh at the way you talk. Maybe they'll be jealous.

D) Failure is the only reason for my depression

I hope you have never thought of success. You are just blaming failures as a reason for your depression. You are giving excuses, and you are not depressed, you are just using depression as an excuse for your failures. The person whose world-changing invention was the result of a 1000 times failures. The bulb was such a great invention that it bred numerous future inventions on its back. When Edison was a child, his teachers called his parents regularly and tell them that their child is weak and can never succeed in life. His teachers were convinced that teaching a brain as slow as his, is a waste of time. But no one knew that this person will invent so many things that people won't forget him even after centuries! And the biggest learning of his success was his 1000 attempts when he failed at his job. But he never stopped; his drive led him to astonishing success and now he is one of the world's most famously successful people. When you feel that you are justified to fail, then there is no use in worrying about it. Don't feel bad about your failures, learn fruitful lessons from them, and try to do something different to make it a success. Dwelling over your failures leads to a loss of motivation.

<u>Have you ever stayed calm even under a lot of pressure?</u>

A) If yes,

You can control your emotions. James Allen says, "the more tranquil a man becomes, the greater is his success, his influence, his power for good." If you are developing the ability to stay calm under pressured situations, you can control your senses and emotions. Staying calm under pressure helps you to improve the ability to focus on the right things to do in your life. You don't want anyone to guide you in your life. So, your pressure capacity allows you to control all your emotions even under lots of challenges. There is none other than you could be even stronger to achieve your destiny. Being calm under pressure required lots of pleasure. Staying calm under pressure helps you to communicate easily with others, and helps your mind to focus on the right things. This quality will make you more intelligent and more effective. Pick these five when you are triggered by pressures. Language is the most powerful weapon in this world. Yes, a good sign of language is peace and happiness. The way you think and speak is the way you become. Swami Vivekananda says, "Talk to yourself at least once in a day... otherwise, you may miss a meeting with an excellent person in this world" we all are unique form each other it also means that we are much better than others in different ways. When you started to communicate with yourself, you can have the power to alter yourself. When you come to know about your inner self, you can easily find solutions for your problems and you try to be calm with yourself.

B) If no,

If your answer is no then I swore that the problem is not with you but the reason for your problem is only you. Yeah, this was little chaos to understand right. Maybe the situation and the people surrounded by you could be the major reason for your problems, but the cause is when you overthink your problems and adding some pepper and salt becomes senseless where you lose your hope. You are confused about what you have planned and what should be executed. And as always you are judging your abilities.

Which wolf do you feed?

Many of us have heard the native American story of two wolves, an old man is teaching his grandson about the life he starts to preach a story "A fight is going on inside me", he said to the boy. it's a terrible fight and it is between two wolves, one is evil. He is anger, sorrow, greed, arrogance, self-pity, guilt, resentment, inferiority, lies, false pride, superiority, and ego. He continued, the other is good he is joy, peace, love, hope, serenity, humility, kindness, benevolence, empathy, generosity, truth, compassion, and faith. The same fight is going on inside of you, and inside of every other person too. After a minute the grandson replied grandpa which wolf wins? The old man simply replied, ***"The one that you feed".***

Now think about yourself. Are you feeding the right wolf? Your subconscious mind always believes what you feed. When you started to feed your mind with positive thoughts, you can attract great things into your life. The only powerhouse of your ability is the positive thoughts you feed to yourself. Train your mind to see the good in the bad. Seed your thoughts with positivity, you can see the garden of positive trees and shrubs within you.

To be pinned!

- I trust myself without any doubt that I'm not imperfect, and I try to see the good in the bad.
- I believe in my ability, and I will overcome my weakness.
- I will focus on my strength.
- I become what I think, I let my thoughts be positive.

When you started to value yourself, then you started to be the best version of yourself. Thoughts you feed the most can create a view upon the better you. Be proud to say "I'm not the copied version of someone". Be yourself do your own thing and work hard and the right things will reach you soon. Yeah, very soon!

VII

Purpose of an internal motivation within you

Purpose starts with your goals and ends with your responsibilities. Every one of us has a unique purpose according to our life. But the insanity lies with our imperfections. Experience, expectations, opinions, and ideas lie within our vision and purpose. *Friedrich Nietzsche* says ***"He who has a why to live for can bear almost any how"*** yeah in your life if you tend to find out why you are here, what was the purpose of your life and tries to understand the goals you pursue, you can suffer through almost any defeat without giving up or quitting. If you have a reason or purpose in life, you can endure almost any misery. Our life has a purpose, but the essence of our life depends upon how soon we acknowledge it. Yeah, like always we are aware of the blueprint that helps us to fulfill our goals and objectives, the question that arises here is, are you really satisfied and happy with what you are right now or else still confused about discovering your path to lead a meaningful life. Are you okay? Keshav chaotically asked his son. Adyen slowly comes near his dad and replies, this is the seventh time you are asking the same question today dad. I've already told you I'm okay... No, my child, you can lie easily but I can understand by seeing your eyes which clearly say that you are missing something and unsatisfied with your life, Am I correct? Adyen with a buzz tone said, "father I am not okay with what I am? Though I am working hard to earn money, and leading a better life with you and mum I can't be satisfied with what I have. I don't understand what I need? And why am I here? Lots of questions with bitterness are messing up into my head". So, what have you decided? Asked Keshav, he said I've saved half of my earnings and I will be back within a year. Where are you going Adyen? In search of happiness, hope my father. Keshav was broken by Adyanth's reply but he accepted his decision for his son's betterment. Adyen traveled a long way. At first, he suffered a lot with his decision, but after a few days, he was happy with it. Because he loves what he does? In search of hope and happiness he went to many places, like temples, tourist spots, hotels, even though he worked in a household shop for a month, but One day when he was sitting in a temple, he tends to see many people helping each other, to keep a step forward to move. He was wondering how confident they are even if they can't walk, some can't see and some can't even recognize what is happening around them. Adyen comes to know about the people there near him were from the sertshang orphanage in Nepal. He was moved by the kindness and he want to do something for them. So, he decided to go to their place and serve them. He learned a lot from them, he doesn't earn a lot of money, and even he'll meet his parents thrice in a year. But he was really happy and satisfied with his purpose. Yeah, after the conversation with his father he traveled towards Nepal and he searched for a job and daily he visited the temple of Buddha, only there he found the purpose of his life. You see in your life it's not a matter of who, from where, and for what you are? If you tend to find out your purpose and are determined to pursue it, it will help you and the people around you anyway. Albert Camus says "Life is the sum of all your choices." So, choose wisely and lead a healthy life.

Ask yourself

My friend always says that ***asking questions is easier than answering those questions***. But according to me asking questions is trickier than answering. I know always you are searching for a why, and so you can learn many things accordingly. If there is no way, when, how, and what, then there is nothing in this world. Bernard M. Baruch says, ***"Millions saw the apple fall, but Newton was the one who asked why."*** When you started to question yourself then it means you are getting ready to accept the changes that lead to success. Could you recollect which was the last day when you questioned yourself? Your mind is essential for your well-being, if you learn to ask why then you can easily succeed anyhow! There are many kinds of stuff to ask yourself, but the fact is you tend to question yourself when you are very weak, and when you did something wrong. If you are questioning yourself when you decide something or when you are very strong then your answers will be a favor for your success. Am I correct? If you are provided with all the benefits, you need and you are not ready to utilize them then you are cheating yourself for futile.

What to ask?

Is this necessary?

This question leads to a yes or no answer. This was a blessing to ask yourself whenever you are in a Stoic situation. It is not easy to question yourself whenever needed because we all are creatures of habit. If we have such a great habit like questioning ourselves then it will help you in your life. In some ways, if you are ready to question yourself, is this necessary then you are mature to guide yourself because most of the time what we decided to do, and think about is not essential for our Purpose. If we are ready to think about it, then you will be provided with lots of time and energy to utilize beneficially. Be a great believer in questioning yourself, because till your death this plays a major role in your life and happiness. Marcus Aurelius says, "Because most of what we say and do is not essential if you can eliminate it, you'll have more time and tranquility. Ask yourself at every moment, ***is this necessary?"***

What to ameliorate?

The best way to ensure what we are doing is all about how we improvised ourselves. Self-improvement avoids a lot of mistakes in our learning process. It helps to enhance our mental and physical health. The never-ending process in our life is to ameliorate oneself. Bernice Johnson Reagan says, "Life's challenges are not supposed to paralyze you, they're supposed to help you discover who you are." According to you the challenges you faced in your life are some more difficult than other people. These challenges are the only icebergs that make some changes in our endeavor.

How to accomplish your dreams and transform them into goals?

Eleanor Roosevelt says, "The future belongs to those who believe in the beauty of their dreams" The only reason to attempt your goals is to follow your dreams. If your dreams are made for your success and happiness, then what is wrong with imagining. But only by imagination and a lot of dreams, we can't attain our success, am I correct? We all know all kinds of definitions when it comes to success. I think you have heard this earlier.

"Dreams won't grind until you execute it" all of us dream a lot but only a few of us chase them until we find it. Jeffrey Gitomer says, "obstacles can't stop you. Most of the other people can't stop you. Only you can stop yourself." Going through hard times is common, but still staying there, results in nothing. C.S. Lewis says, "you can't go back and change the beginning, but you can start where you are and change the ending" the only message that you should believe each day is you, yeah, you are worth for what you deserve. You are the only person who should value you. If you are getting caught in the same situation, again and again, remember that the situation is trying to tell you something that you want to know. But the problem here is you have no time to listen and analyze what you want to learn from those circumstances. Commonly there are four pillars in our life,

- Purpose of belief.
- Purpose of sadness.
- Purpose of problems.

- Purpose of action.

Could you guess what these four pillars trying to tell us, they are just stopped by a brick. Let me throw light upon your guess right now, A successful young man with his brand new car was riding down a neighborhood rural street. When he noticed a boy darting out between many other parked cars. He slowed down a little as he appeared nearby. Suddenly a brick smashed into his car's door. He slammed on the brakes and drove back to the place where the brick had been thrown. The ferocious man jiggled out of his car and caught the boy and he yelled, "what have you done to my car? Why did you do it?" The young boy was a little scared but was very elegant and apologetic. "I am sorry, Mister. I didn't know what else to do, he pleaded. I had to throw the brick because no one else would stop me for my calling to help." With tears rolling down his cheeks he pointed towards the parked cars and said it's my mom she rolled off the curb and fell off his wheelchair and she was badly hurt. I can't lift her. The sobbing kid asked the businessman would you please help me get her back into her wheelchair she's hurt and she's too heavy for me the businessman was moved beyond words and try to control his emotions towards him spelling lump in his throat Then he hurriedly litter his mother from the spot and put her back in the wheelchair. He also helped the boy to admit his mom to the hospital with small injuries. When he thought that everything would be OK he went back to his car thank you, Sir and God, bless you said the grateful kid the end man was too shaken up for any word so the man watched the little boy push his mom who uses a wheelchair down the sidewalk it was a long and slow ride back home to the man when he came out of the car he looked at his dented car door the damage was very noticeable but he does not bother to repair it instead he kept the dent to remind him of the message ***" Do not go through life so fast that someone has to throw a brick at you to get your attention"*** doesn't this story melts your heart, and could you guess how those four pillars connected to this story? Actually, Life whispers in our souls and speaks with us it just yells, Sometimes when you do not tend to listen to what is happening around you life throws a brick at us it's our choice to listen to it or wait for the brick. Our own beliefs, sadness, problems, and actions are the reflections of what we do, how we think, and how we react? It is all about where we stand and how we erupt!

VIII

conclusion

Stephen King once said, ***“Get busy living or get busy dying”*** we all have 86,400 seconds each day and it’s our own choice to enhance them properly. We all are not forced to behave perfectly but at times we tend to do so. If you want yourself to be the best, then you should strive hard to achieve at least something. One cannot build self-esteem while doing nothing. The more idea time we have doesn’t help us because it causes our mind to be valued not to be focused on something about the situation that we are actually in. what I'm saying is ***"A good start commences a good ending"***. All the above chapters about how to plan and pursue everything that you are indicated, the purpose of an internal motivation within you, how to practice beyond necessities, what are the miracle powers you indulged, and self-observation will help you to find out what lags with you? and makes a strong sense to plan on navigating your life, but after some long days, you should not lose track of scrutinizing yourself which is very important during the journey of your life.

what is the message?

This book depicts some important messages that could mean a great takeaway for you, my readers. This will make you functional. This time you are going to rule yourself more perfectly after completing this book. Let me project some important facts, in short, to enhance yourself that I've told you in the above chapter's in detail.

Being tenacious

Abraham Lincoln says, **"when you reach the end of your rope, tie a knot and hang on".** Being tenacious is nothing but being determined, and not accepting your failures easily. You should mold yourself into the baggage of a determining person. If you are determined to do anything then it is a good trait to develop. When development acquires, you automatically get to know what's next? The development process within you will take failures as challenges and force you to work harder to reach your destiny. To execute your tasks to be summarized today itself. Allow your mind to think about what you will be achieved

Experience- good teacher

I've already said, " Experience makes you nonpareil". It's not important how long you learn, but it's all about what you learn, and with that experience what you have achieved is very much important. There is a short saying by an unknown author about the experience,

" Sir what is the secret to your success?" a reporter asked the bank manager.

" Two words"
"And sir what are they?"
"Good decision"
"And how do you make good decisions?"
" One word".
" And sir what is that?"
"Experience."
"And how did you get to experience"
"Two words."
"And sir what are they?"
"Bad decisions."

If you ask me what makes you a mature person, I'll say it is your own experience and the decisions you make in your life. From today on, take an oath, you will make a decision which may be tough and perhaps which leads you to be stressed but you will tend to learn a lot of things to be succeeded. Let me tell you a secret it is all within you!

Printed by Libri Plureos GmbH in Hamburg,
Germany